The Adventures of Scuba Jack
Copyright 2022 by Beth Costanzo
All rights reserved

Let's go down to the ocean blue.
Lots of things to see and do!

Down at the seashore I dig with my hands and wiggle my toes in the soft warm sand.

The seashore's a beautiful treasure chest.
Finding sparkly shells is always the best.

I hear the children laugh and shout,
as they play and run, and clammer about.

A wave comes splashing over my toes.
I stand still and away it goes.

A Hermit Crab needs a new home.
The one he has he's already outgrown.

A lighthouse shines bright in the night.
It helps ships navigate by glowing bright.

Seagulls soar up in the sky.
A little crab pauses, then scampers by.

Pools of water stay in rocks at low tide.
These tidal pools are where creatures hide.

Splashing in the water of the cool blue sea,
I play wave tag. "You can't catch me!"

I jump in the waves, swim, play, and run.
Building sandcastles is so much fun.

The sun is setting. It's time to go.
The fireflies are dancing to and fro.

I can't wait to return to the ocean blue.
Lots of things to see and do!